DATE DUE			

FLYING START

RUNNING

Lew Emmence

The Bookwright Press
New York • 1992

Flying Start

Titles in this series

Fishing	Running
Gymnastics	Soccer
Judo	Swimming

Words in **bold** in the text are explained in the glossary on page 30.

Cover: Young racers in a close finish.

First published in the
United States in 1992 by
The Bookwright Press
387 Park Avenue South
New York, NY 10016

First published in 1991 by
Wayland (Publishers) Ltd
61 Western Rd, Hove
East Sussex BN3 1JD, England

© Copyright 1991 Wayland (Publishers) Ltd

Library of Congress Cataloging-in-Publication Data
Emmence, Lew
    Running/by Lew Emmence.
        p.   cm.—(Flying start)
    Includes index
    Summary: Examines running as a sport, including the equipment
    needed and training for competitions.
        ISBN 0–531–18464–1
        1. Running—Juvenile literature.   [1. Running.]   I. Series.
    GV1061.E45   1991   91–15143
    796.42—dc20   CIP
                                                                        AC

Typesetter: Dorchester Typesetting Group Ltd
Printer: G. Canale C.S.p.A., Turin

CONTENTS

FIRST STEPS

The photograph on the right shows the New York Marathon. Every year thousands of runners enjoy proving they can run 26.22 miles (42.2 km). The first marathon was not a race, but the distance a Greek soldier called Pheidippides had to run to Athens. He was delivering news that the Greek army had defeated the Persians at the Battle of Marathon in 490 BC.

Running is the most popular sport in the world. The story of running goes back in history to the days when hunters needed to be able to track animals to eat.

You do not need expensive equipment for running. It is difficult to play team games unless you have

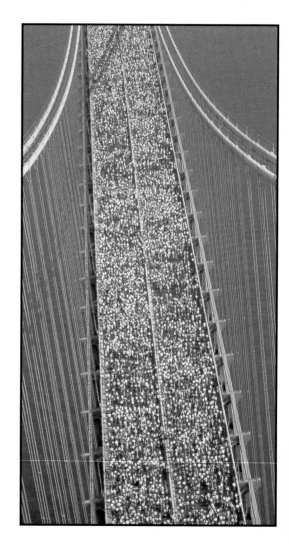

a team and opponents, but you can run on your own. You may aim to run a bit farther each week or run faster between two markers.

Running across country can be more fun than running around a track.

When you hear people talk about running they may mean a number of different things. You can **sprint**, run **long distances** or anything in between. You can run on a track, a road or across country. Whatever you choose, running is fun and good practice for other games.

The steeplechase is for older athletes – the water jump is a real test of courage.

This girl is in a relay race, in which each member of the team runs a section. They pass the baton (which she is holding in her right hand) between them.

Some runners want to be the fastest in races, but for most runners the sport is fun and a very good way to keep fit. So, let's find out how you can enjoy the oldest sport in the world.

If you want to run faster, what you think is as important as how much you run. For many years runners thought it was impossible to run a mile (1.6 km) in less than four minutes. So nobody did. But in 1954 a young English runner named Roger Bannister told himself that the four minute mile must be possible. His friends helped him to train, and Roger managed to run a mile in 3 minutes 59.4 seconds. Afterward, many runners ran even faster than that, because they knew it was possible to do so!

Today, mile races are unusual. It is much more common to race over 1,500 meters, which is a little less than a mile.

Above Nelli Cooman of Holland – World Indoor 60 m Champion in 1968.

Left Being able to run quickly is important in lots of sports, among them soccer.

You may like other sports better than running, but stop and think. In how many other sports do you need to be a good runner? Volleyball, soccer, basketball, baseball . . . I am sure you could add plenty more. Boxers run every day as part of their training.

We usually think about running as going fast, but many runners enjoy running slowly. This is usually called **jogging**. Many families jog together, in the woods or in parks or on local sidewalks.

If you want to be one of the fast runners, there are rules to remember before you can be successful:

- Run where it is safe.
- Never run on the road.
- Get your body used to exercise gradually.
- Do not expect to improve in every race without training.
- Warm up before any hard running.
- Never run at your fastest pace before warming up.
- Do not try to run so far that you feel ill afterward.

Left Jogging is fun.

Above Always run on the sidewalk – the road is very dangerous.

Look after your body by eating the right foods, even if these are not your favorites. You should eat lots of different types of food: meat, vegetables, fruit and cereals.

Athletes often use the words warmup and training. What do they mean?

Above Warm up well before training and racing, or you risk being injured.

Your body needs to be prepared for hard exercise by using all your muscles gently at first. If you watch an international athlete warming up, you will see that he or she has a set of exercises to go through. They are always used before training or racing. This is the warmup. Always warm up all your muscles, from your neck down to your toes.

A runner warming up his leg muscles. This exercise is useful for hurdlers, who get into a similar position as they take the hurdle.

Training is preparing over a long period of time to go as fast as you can. International runners and their coaches plan work for each day of the week. Long distance runners run farthest in training, but all runners practice, or train, by running shorter distances than they will run in competitions. They do this so that they can get used to running faster.

To train, runners do a set number of runs, repeated at set intervals. So a runner may aim to run 165 yd (150 m) six times, each in 25 seconds. In between he or she rests for 30 seconds while jogging very slowly. Playing games like tag and touch football are good practice for running.

There are lots of ways to train. Your coach has to decide on the best way to train for the event and distance you want to race over.

You will not have to train this way until you are much older.

long jump in one afternoon. He went on to win four gold medals at the **Olympic Games** in 1936.

If you improve your running you often become better at other athletic events. In 1935 at Ohio State University, a student named Jesse Owens startled everyone by setting world records for the 100 yd dash, the 220 yd dash, the 220 yd low hurdles and the

Starting

Before going to the starting line, check that your shoelaces are tied tightly.

On your mark!
Get set!
Go!

This is what you will hear at the start of a race. What should you do at each stage?

When there are this many people starting the race, you have to be careful not to get knocked down.

"On your mark!" Move to the starting line. Use a standing position, which is better than a crouch position. Put your front toe as close to the starting line as possible (you must not touch the line). Your front leg should be bent and most of your weight on your front foot. Your back foot should be 12 to 16 in (30–40 cm) behind your front one. Stand with your arms relaxed and lean slightly forward. Keep still.

"Get set!" Concentrate on what you must do when you start running. Look forward at where you are going to run, not at the starter. Have one arm slightly forward (the one opposite your front foot).

"Go!" Push hard with your back leg. Swing your rear arm forward and keep your body low for the first few strides. Starting early is called a **false start**.

"On your mark . . .

"Get set . . .

"Go!"

17

Florence Griffith Joyner, U.S. Olympic gold medalist, running upright and looking relaxed.

Smart running

If athletes are running around a track, they have to stay in their lanes. Those on the inside start behind those on the outside. This is called a **stagger**. At the end of a lap each runner will have run the same distance. When running around a track, stay close to the inside of your lane, so that you run the shortest distance possible. If you run around a track in a group, the athletes on the inside run a shorter distance than those on the outside.

Sprinting

Run upright, without leaning forward. Keep your eyes looking a long way ahead, whenever possible past the finishing line. Lift your knees up high, but do not **overstride**. Drive with your arms: "The faster the arms, the faster the legs."

A staggered start. The runners on the outside of the track would have to run farther than those on the inside if they all started in the same place. That is because it is farther around the outside edge of a bend. So those on the outside start in front of the runners on the inside, and they all run the same distance.

Middle distance

You need to save your strength, so do not put as much power into your arms and legs. You will not be able to keep it up. Try to keep to an even pace, except at the end of the race, when you should sprint for the line. Do not get **boxed** in the center of a group of runners, or you might get stuck behind them.

Finishing

No matter how far you have run, you finish when your body (not arms or legs) crosses the finish line. Even famous runners lose races if they look around and are overtaken. Run through the finish line and 30 ft (9 m) past it to make sure you do not get overtaken at the end.

Left A close finish. Who do you think won? (Find out on page 32.)

Above The runner wearing black is boxed behind the leaders.

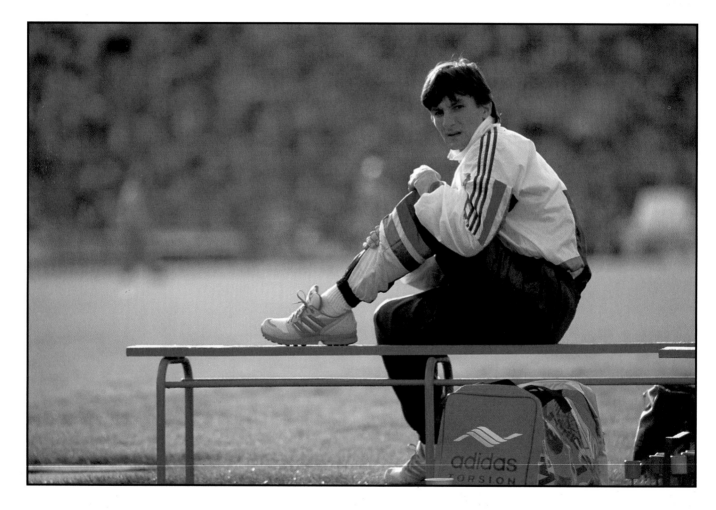

Above A Romanian athlete, keeping warm in a track suit.

You do not have to wear colorful one-piece suits like the ones Carl Lewis and other runners wear. These outfits look good, but will not make you into a champion.

The most important thing to remember is keep warm. That is why runners wear track suits until just before the start of a race. Unless it is very cold, shorts and a cotton T-shirt are the most comfortable clothes to run in.

Running shoes are the most sensible things to wear on your feet. Some top athletes wear spiked shoes, but these can be dangerous. Footwear is the most important item. Lace-up shoes are essential, with the soles built up to keep you from jarring your spine. The heels should be low enough to allow movement at the ankle. Go to a runners' store, not a fashion store, to buy shoes.

British sprinter Linford Christie often wears long pants to keep his legs warm.

Competitions have taken place for thousands of years. The first races were probably the ancient Olympic Games. The modern Olympic Games started in 1896 and are held

Your first race will not be in front of a big crowd, but you will still be nervous.

This girl has learned to hurdle very well.

in a different country every four years. In both ancient and modern Games, running events have been among the most popular. Olympic champions become famous throughout the world. To be a champion you must enjoy running in front of millions of people.

First come the years of training so that you can run fast enough to be invited to race. Then comes the excitement, building up until the day of the competition.

Being excited before a competition affects each person in a different way. Some of the common ways excitement shows are:

- Not being able to sleep the night before the race.
- Not feeling hungry, or perhaps feeling hungry all the time.
- Wanting to go to the toilet a lot.
- Biting your fingernails.

Whether it is your first competition or the final of the Olympic Games you will always feel strange. If you do not feel a bit nervous you will probably not run very well.

Below Waiting for the baton to be passed in a relay.

When you enter a race there are several tips you could take from international athletes.

- Do not eat just before a race.
- Warm up well, by doing the exercises worked out with your coach.
- Concentrate hard on what you have to do. Do not let yourself be distracted.

Do you remember to warm up for every run, like British sprinter Linford Christie?

27

Sebastian Coe knows how it feels to be a runner in school races as well as Olympic Games and World Championships. He was the first person to win the 1,500 m at two Olympic Games, in Moscow (1980) and Los Angeles (1984). Besides

As soon as he crossed the line, Sebastian Coe started celebrating his second Olympic gold medal for 1,500 m. He won for Britain in 1980 and 1984.

being a winner he was very fast, and he set 800-m, mile and 1,500-m records. At school Sebastian had run longer distances and was English Schools Champion at 3,000 m.

Being able to run fast is a useful skill in many sports. So even if you do not want to be Sebastian Coe or Florence Griffith Joyner, how about getting into running?

How about getting into running? You are never too young to start.

Glossary

Boxed Stuck in the middle of a group of runners and unable to get out.

False start A false start is called when someone starts running before the gun goes off. If this happens to you three times you will not be allowed to be in the race.

Jogging Running slowly (somewhere between running and walking speed).

Long distance Races from 3,000 m (3,280 yd) to marathon length.

Middle distance Races from 800 m to 3,000 m (875 – 3,280 yd) in length.

Olympic Games A sports competition held every four years, in different cities around the world.

Overstride To take running steps that are too long and high.

Sprint Races from 60 m (65 yd) (indoors) to 400 m (437 yd) in length.

Stagger The stagger at the start of a race is designed to make sure that the athletes in different lanes all run the same distance. The runners on the outside start in front of those on the inside, because they have a bigger bend to run.

Books to read

Aaseng, Nathan. *Track's Magnificent Milers* (Lerner Publications, 1981)
Dickmeyer, Lowell A. *A Track Is for Me* (Lerner Publications, 1979)
Gutman, Bill. *Go For It: Track & Field* (Grey Castles, 1989)
McMane, Fred. *Track & Field Basics* (Prentice Hall, 1983)
Peach, S. *Running Skills* (EDC Publishing, 1988)

Acknowledgments

The artwork on page 17 was provided by Peter Parr.

The publishers would like to thank the following for permission to reproduce their photographs in this book: All-Sport *cover*, 5 (Kirk Schlea), 6 (Tony Duffy), 7 (not credited), 8 (Richiardi), 9 (Steve Powell), 10 (Kirk Schlea), 11 (Ancil Nance), 13 (Mike Powell), 14 (Steve Powell), 15 (not credited), 16 (Howard Boylan), 18 (Gerard Vandystad), 19 (Gray Mortimore), 20 (Mike Powell), 21 (Dan Smith), 22 (Mike Powell), 23 (Dan Smith), 24 (Tony Duffy), 25 (Roger Labrosse), 26 (Bob Martin), 27 (Gray Mortimore), 28 (Steve Powell), 29 (Bob Martin); Eye Ubiquitous 12; Zefa 4.

The next step

When writing for material, send a stamped, self-addressed envelope.

United States
Amateur Athletic Union of the United States
3400 W. 86th Street
Indianapolis
Indiana 46268

Road Runners Club of America
629 S. Washington Street
Alexandria
Virginia 22314

Canada
Canadian Track & Field Association
1600 James Naismith Drive
Gloucester
Ontario K1B 5N4

Index

Greg Foster (dressed in black) beat Roger Kingdom in the finish on page 20.